W9-AFG-714

Calvin Klein

Fashion Design Superstar

By Diane Dakers

Crabtree Publishing Company
www.crabtreebooks.com

Crabtree Publishing Company

www.crabtreebooks.com

Author: Diane Dakers
Publishing plan research and development:
  Sean Charlebois, Reagan Miller
  Crabtree Publishing Company
Editors: Mark Sachner, Lynn Peppas
Proofreader: Wendy Scavuzzo
Indexer: Wendy Scavuzzo
Editorial director: Kathy Middleton
Photo researcher: Ruth Owen
Designer: Alix Wood
Production coordinator: Margaret Amy Salter
Production: Kim Richardson
Prepress technician: Margaret Amy Salter

Written, developed, and produced by
Water Buffalo Books

Publisher's note:
All quotations in this book come from original sources and contain the spelling and grammatical inconsistencies of the original text. The use of such constructions is for the sake of preserving the historical and literary accuracy of the sources.

Photographs and reproductions:
Alamy: Lewton Cole: front cover (main); front cover (background); Lewton Cole; page 4 (inset); Lewton Cole: page 15
Corbis: Condé Nast Archive Flickr: 24; Pierre Schermann: 39; Pierre Schermann: page 53
(Creative Commons): page 1; page 4 (background); page 5; page 13; page 29; page 32 (all); page 45; page 46; page 51; page 60; page 63; page 65; page 70; page 71; page 75; page 88; page 93; page 96; page 103 (left); page 103 (center)
Getty Images: Stuart Ramson: page 7; Ke. Mazur: page 59; Ron Galella: page 67; New York Daily News: page 68; Rose Hartman: page 73; Rose Hartman: page 85; Adam Rountree: page 95. Public domain: page 23; page 47
Paramount Pictures/Keystone Press: page 81
Rex Features: News UK Ltd: page 77
Shutterstock: page 9; pages 10-11 (background); page 16; page 19; page 22; page 26; page 27; page 35; page 37; page 40; page 41; page 44; page 54; page 57; page 82; page 83; page 87; page 89; page 103
Wikipedia (public domain): page 11 (inset); page 31; page 49; page 99 (all)

Cover: Truly the first fashion design superstar, Calvin Klein has set the standard over the last four decades for elegant sportswear and simple, free-flowing eveningwear. Even his name has become something to wear. The famous button logo on Calvin Klein jeans is recognized around the world.

Library and Archives Canada Cataloguing in Publication

Dakers, Diane
      Calvin Klein : fashion design superstar / Diane Dakers.

(Crabtree groundbreaker biographies)
Includes index.
Issued also in an electronic format.
ISBN 978-0-7787-2534-3 (bound).--ISBN 978-0-7787-2543-5 (pbk.)

      1. Klein, Calvin, 1942- --Juvenile literature. 2. Fashion designers--United States--Biography--Juvenile literature.
I. Title. II. Series: Crabtree groundbreaker biographies

TT505.K54 D33 2011   j746.9'2092   C2010-903020-6

Library of Congress Cataloging-in-Publication Data

Dakers, Diane.
      Calvin Klein : fashion design superstar / Diane Dakers.
        p. cm. -- (Crabtree groundbreaker biographies)
      Includes index.
      ISBN 978-0-7787-2543-5 (pbk. : alk. paper) --
      ISBN 978-0-7787-2534-3 (reinforced library binding : alk. paper) -- ISBN 978-1-4271-9466-4 (electronic (PDF))
      1. Klein, Calvin, 1942---Juvenile literature. 2. Fashion designers--United States--Biography--Juvenile literature.
      I. Title. II. Series.

      TT505.K58D35 2011
      746.9'2092--dc22
      [B]
                                                      2010018042

Crabtree Publishing Company

www.crabtreebooks.com   1-800-387-7650

Printed in the USA/082010/BL20100723

Published in Canada
Crabtree Publishing
616 Welland Ave.
St. Catharines, Ontario
L2M 5V6

Published in the United States
Crabtree Publishing
PMB 59051
350 Fifth Avenue, 59th Floor
New York, New York 10118

Published in the United Kingdom
Crabtree Publishing
Maritime House
Basin Road North, Hove
BN41 1WR

Published in Australia
Crabtree Publishing
386 Mt. Alexander Rd.
Ascot Vale (Melbourne)
VIC 3032

Chapter 3 First Forays into Fashion 29

Chapter 4 The '70s and '80s—The Rising Star 51

Chapter 5 The 1990s—The Fall and Rise
of Calvin Klein 75

Chapter 6 Calvin Klein in the 21st Century—
The Icon Steps Aside 93

Chronology 104

Glossary 106

Further Information 108

Index 110

About the Author 112

Chapter 1
The Man Makes the Style

For weeks in the spring of 1968, young Calvin Klein camped out in Room 613 of the nondescript York Hotel in New York City's Fashion District, desperate to make some sales. With his first fashion collection hung on racks by his side, the 25-year-old worked the phones day after day, calling potential customers and fashion writers, urging them to come see the six coats and three dresses he had designed.

Custin was so taken with the collection, she placed a $50,000 order on the spot, launching Calvin Klein's career.

Opposite: The Calvin Klein label has long been a sign of cool, comfortable, and affordable fashion.

Right Place, Right Time

At the time, the York Hotel served as an unofficial fashion marketplace for clothing sellers and designers who converted the dreary guest rooms into mini-showrooms to display their wares to potential buyers.

Calvin's room was perfectly positioned across from the elevator. When the elevator doors opened, any visitor to the sixth floor had a perfect view to his collection through the open door of Room 613.

One day, an executive from the upscale department store Bonwit Teller was on his way to an appointment on one of the York Hotel's upper floors. For some reason, the elevator accidentally opened on the sixth floor, and the man got a glimpse of Calvin's collection.

The executive continued on to his appointment but, on his way back down, he stopped for a closer look at the young designer's work. Impressed with what he saw, he invited Calvin to present his collection a few days later to Bonwit Teller president Mildred Custin, the queen bee of the fashion industry.

Custin was so taken with the collection, she placed a $50,000 order on the spot, launching Calvin Klein's career.

From that moment on, for the next 40 years—until his final fashion show in 2003—Calvin Klein would be one of the brightest lights in the American fashion world, creating an impact on everything from undies to advertising.

During his career, he would change the way North Americans felt about three everyday products—jeans, underwear, and perfume.

Models walk the runway at the Calvin Klein Spring/Summer 2004 Collection show at Bryant Park in New York City during the 7th on Sixth Mercedes-Benz Fashion Week on September 16, 2003.

Before he came along, these were pretty standard items that didn't warrant a second thought.

Today, thanks to Calvin Klein, jeans are worn everywhere, from the grocery store to the red carpet; underpants come in hundreds of colors and styles; and men and women share some of the same bottled scents.

Emblazoned on all of these products and more is the name of the man whose concepts of design and of "branding" product lines would shake up the worlds of fashion and advertising alike.

A Man of Style

Throughout his career, Calvin Klein's clothing has been described as simple, clean, sleek, understated, and elegant; casual but sophisticated; even, for those given to using smart-sounding words to describe simple concepts, "the quintessence of American fashion expression and taste."

"The Calvin Klein Look," as it is called, is about more than just the style of the clothing. In creating this signature look, Calvin also created a new attitude toward fashion, a thread that is seen through all his collections through all his years as a designer. By pairing unexpected weaves, fabrics, and creative elements, he gave people a way to be comfortable and fashionable at the same time.

He made casual garments, like T-shirts, jackets, and blouses, out of soft, luxurious fabrics such as silk, cashmere, and satin. He focused on natural, neutral, earthy colors and no-frills fashions that suit all body shapes and sizes. He was one of the first designers to make elegant sportswear and simple, free-flowing eveningwear.

In short, wearing Calvin Klein made a person cool.

Bound for Greatness

For the innovation and creativity of his collections, Calvin earned award after award during his design career. In 2001, he earned the ultimate honor, a Lifetime Achievement Award from the Council of Fashion Designers of America.

Of course, at that chance meeting at the York Hotel in 1968, the young designer from the Bronx, the son of a grocery store worker, had no idea that one day, the whole world would know his name. He couldn't have imagined that he would be a multi-millionaire by the time he was 40, would be as famous as a Hollywood movie star, or would become one of the most successful American fashion designers in history.

Back at the York Hotel in 1968, Calvin Klein was just a young man who loved fashion and believed that designing clothing was what he was born to do. He had a vision for what he wanted to create and, even then, he did what he had to do—defying rules and standing his ground—to make his vision a reality.

FROM DUNGAREES TO DESIGNER DUDS

There was a time when denim dungarees—what we call blue jeans—were only worn by miners, farmers, and cowboys. Today, almost everyone owns at least one pair of jeans, and they're no longer just for hard work.

Made from heavy woven cotton fabric, jeans were invented by Levi Strauss in 1853. A Jewish immigrant from Germany who set up shop in San Francisco during the gold rush, Strauss sold canvas for tents and wagon covers. When one of his customers, a gold prospector, suggested that Strauss make pants instead of tents, Strauss started sewing what he called waist overalls. Then, because the canvas was too rough, he changed to a heavy cotton fabric from France, called "serge de Nimes," a name later shortened to denim.

Twenty years later, the pants still had one problem—the back pockets ripped away too easily. Jacob Davis, a tailor from Nevada, found a solution: to attach the pockets with metal rivets. With no money to patent his idea, Davis asked Levi Strauss to help finance it. On May 20, 1873, Strauss and Davis got their patent, and blue jeans were born.

In the 1930s, the tough trousers were worn by cowboys in Western movies; during World War II, off-duty American servicemen often wore dungarees; and in the 1950s, Hollywood movie stars like James Dean in the movie *Rebel Without a Cause* popularized the pants with teenagers. In 1978, Calvin Klein was one of the first designers to brand jeans with his name on the back pocket.

Copper rivets, born out of necessity as a way of securing the back pockets of early dungarees, are now an accepted feature in the design of most jeans.

By the 1950s, blue jeans, with or without the cuffs rolled, were part of a "look" identified with tough, troubled youth.

Chapter 2
Growing Up in Style

He may have ended up living the glam life of an international fashion icon, but Calvin Klein's early years in no way gave any hint of the glossy journey that was to come. Born into a working-class Jewish family, Calvin Klein understood from his early childhood that the better things in life did not come without hard work.

Immigrant Roots
Calvin Richard Klein was born in New York City, in the Bronx, on November 19, 1942, to Leo, who had emigrated from Hungary as a child, and Flore, the daughter of an Austrian immigrant and an American dentist. Both parents held jobs. Flo worked at a grocery store

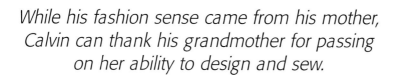

While his fashion sense came from his mother, Calvin can thank his grandmother for passing on her ability to design and sew.

near the family's home, while Leo commuted into Manhattan to Harlem, where he put in long hours at the grocery store he owned. Eventually, poor health forced Leo to close his store. He spent the rest of his career working at his brother's more successful grocery business, Ernest Klein & Co., a supermarket that continues to thrive in Manhattan today.

Flo was crazy for fashion and bought new outfits every week.

The Klein family—including Calvin's older brother Barry and younger sister Alexis—lived in close quarters in a standard apartment in the Mosholu Parkway area of the Bronx. A lively melting pot of cultures, mostly Eastern European, Irish, and Italian, Mosholu Parkway was a hard-working, middle-class community, full of trees and fresh air. Despite the Jewish immigrant heritage he shared with many of the other children in his neighborhood, young Calvin didn't quite fit in.

A Budding Fashion Sense

Young Calvin was a skinny kid less interested in playing after-school sports with the neighborhood boys than he was in hanging out with his grandmother in her dress and

Even as an accomplished, world-famous superstar in the realm of fashion design, Calvin credited his grandmother, Molly Stern, for instilling in him the basics of sewing as a key component of design. Here he is shown in 1985, working with fabric on a dress form.

notions shop. From his mother, he inherited a love of the finer things in life. Flo was crazy for fashion and bought new outfits every week, scouting out designer labels at discount prices.

Flo also made sure her son was always well turned-out in the sharpest, most dashing attire. Even in kindergarten, little Calvin was dressed in perfectly washed and ironed, unusually colored shirts—pink, mauve, and purple—with little bow ties.

While the other kids wore plain pants and sneakers, Calvin, always the trendsetter, shopped in Manhattan and dressed in the latest fashion.

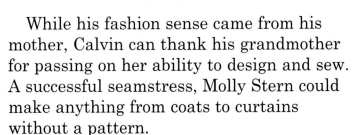

While his fashion sense came from his mother, Calvin can thank his grandmother for passing on her ability to design and sew. A successful seamstress, Molly Stern could make anything from coats to curtains without a pattern.

Young Calvin worshiped his grandma and her craft. In fact, he was so fascinated with sewing that his mother gave him a sewing machine for one of his early birthdays.

The little boy loved making clothes, so much so that he once designed an entire wardrobe

> *"She loved beautiful clothes, and she had no sense of money," Calvin once said about his mother, Flore Klein. "She was outrageous in her day. She'd have white fleece suits lined with black Persian lamb—when you think of the Bronx, you don't think of clothes like that. We weren't really wealthy, but she managed. My father was ... a great guy who allowed his wife to spend their money on clothes."*

for his sister's friends' dolls. Later, he tried his hand at sewing dresses for Flo, who completely supported her son in his unusual pastime. Leo wasn't as crazy about his boy's passion for fashion—but, a quiet and reserved man, he didn't push his views on Calvin.

Not surprisingly, his crafty hobby made Calvin an oddball in the neighborhood. Kids teased him, but it didn't faze him one bit:

> *"I never went through the thing most young people do, going to school and not truly knowing what they want to do until later in life. I had a major head start. At age five, I had a pretty good idea of what I wanted to do."*

Fast Friends

It was also at age five that Calvin met Barry Schwartz, who was six months older and would become his lifelong friend and business partner.

Like Calvin's father, Barry's dad owned a grocery store in Harlem. Every day, Leo Klein and Harry Schwartz commuted by train to their respective stores—that's how they met and became friendly. Eventually, the men introduced their young sons, and the boys became best friends.

The little boy loved making clothes, so much so that he once designed an entire wardrobe for his sister's friends' dolls.

Even as kids, Calvin and Barry were always coming up with new ways to earn money. At six, they opened an iced tea stand on the street; at eight, they bought newspapers and sold each copy at a two-cent mark-up. The little boys dreamed about opening their own supermarket one day.

School Days

In the tough, struggling Mosholu Parkway neighborhood in general, and in the Klein

PS 80:
CELEBRITY SCHOOL

Calvin Klein wasn't the only celebrity fashion
designer to hail from PS 80 in the Mosholu Parkway
neighborhood. Ralph Lauren attended the school
for a few years but transferred to a traditional Jewish
school for an Orthodox Jewish education after grade
two. Because Lauren is three years older than Calvin,
the two designers attended PS 80 a few years apart
and never met as schoolchildren.

Actor and director Penny Marshall (of *Laverne
and Shirley* fame) and her brother Garry Marshall
(creator of *Happy Days* and director of *Runaway
Bride, The Princess Diaries,* and
Raising Helen) also attended
PS 80.

household in particular, education was a high priority. It was understood that a good education was the ticket to better things in life, a professional career, a fine income, and the promise of a better time of it for one's kids.

Calvin took his education seriously and did well at school, earning As and Bs in every class. His best subjects were drawing and art. In fact, Calvin was so artistically talented, he was asked to paint a mural in the fifth-floor hallway just outside the principal's office at his school, PS 80. At age 12, he joined the Art Students League, traveling to Manhattan every Saturday to participate in extra sketching and drawing classes.

During his public school years, Calvin's individual style continued to develop. While the other kids wore plain pants and sneakers, Calvin, always the trendsetter, shopped in Manhattan and dressed in the latest fashion.

Strangely, he and his best friend, Barry, never went to the same school. Even though the families lived just two blocks apart, Barry's home was in a different school district. He attended PS 56, while Calvin attended PS 80.

When it came time for high school, most of the neighborhood boys—including Barry—attended DeWitt Clinton High School, a boys-only school in the area. Fourteen-year-old Calvin decided to attend the High School of Industrial Art in Manhattan, a subway ride away. "I couldn't wait to get to high school so that I could get out of the Bronx," he said.

HIGH SCHOOL OF FAME

Other famous graduates of the High School
of Industrial Art, Calvin's alma mater, include
legendary crooner Tony Bennett (class of '45),
Pulitzer Prize-winning graphic novelist and
creator of the autobiographical comic book *Maus:
A Survivor's Tale*, Art Spiegelman (class of '65),
Paul Charles Caravello, better known as Eric Carr,
drummer for the rock band KISS (class of '67),
and fashion designer Marc Jacobs (class of '81).

FASHION INSTITUTE OF TECHNOLOGY

Founded in 1944 with 100 students attending classes on
the top two floors of the High School of Needle Trades,
FIT now takes up an entire city block at the edge of New
York's fabulous Garment District. More than 10,000
students study such programs as Accessories Design,
Menswear, Cosmetics and Fragrance Marketing, Fashion
Merchandising, Fabric Styling Management, Illustration,
Photography, and, of course, Fashion Design.

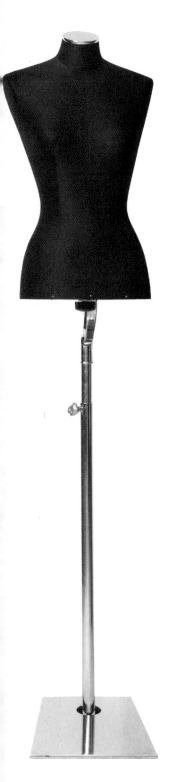

Making the Move to Manhattan

While his personal pizzazz and artistic flair stuck out like a sore thumb in the Bronx and at PS 80, Calvin blended right in at the High School of Industrial Art, where he majored in fashion illustration. After his graduation, the 17-year-old continued on the fashion-design track, enrolling at the Fashion Institute of Technology (FIT), one of New York's top design schools.

Calvin was immediately bored at FIT. He found the first-year trade-oriented courses mind numbing and stifling, so he created his own course of study on the side, focusing on fashion designers he admired. Two in particular caught the young student's attention—French-born Jacques Tiffeau and American Claire McCardell.

Calvin found FIT so uninspiring that he quit school after his first year, figuring he would get a job in the fashion biz, get a foot in a door, and launch his design career that way instead.

He did get a job—as a copy boy, or errand boy—at *Women's Wear Daily*, the main fashion magazine of the day. He started on May 8, 1961, an ambitious young man like so many others in the industry. In the end, nobody took any particular notice of the copy boy and, six months later, the 19-year-old quit his job. He returned to FIT, plodded through another year, and graduated in January 1962. His disrespect for the program was such that he did not attend his graduation ceremony; nor did he sit for a yearbook photo. His legacy at the school is marked by a typo in the class yearbook, where he is listed as "Alvin Klein."

Claire McCardell:
Groundbreaking Female Designer

Considered the founder of ready-to-wear fashion in the United States, Claire McCardell created a loose, relaxed style in the 1940s known as "the American Look." A former model and one of the few female American designers of her day, McCardell knew what women wanted and needed—fashions that were comfortable but chic, sophisticated but functional. "Most of my ideas come from trying to solve my own problems," said McCardell, who introduced free-flowing, comfortable garments to American women.

Her first major success came in 1938 when she created a popular shapeless tent dress that could be tied to fit any woman's body. A few years later, in 1942, she introduced a new style—a wrap-around denim dress, or jumper, designed to be worn over top of other clothes.

McCardell experimented with unusual fabrics, using denim for dresses, wool for evening wear, tweed for coats, and cotton for swimsuits. She loved leotards, hoods, Capri pants, and full, gathered skirts. She used crazy color combinations, promoted the ballet slipper as a street shoe, and invented the concept of mix-and-match separates.

The Maryland-born designer's work has been so influential that, in 1990, *Life* magazine named her one of the 100 most important Americans of the twentieth century. In 1994, the *New York Times* dubbed her "this country's finest designer."

McCardell died of cancer in 1958 at age 52.

Two models are shown wearing Claire McCardell dresses fashioned out of identical floral-print fabric. One dress is short, and the other has a longer-length design, inspired by designer Christian Dior. Both dresses have the full, gathered skirts that were a signature feature of McCardell's work.

School Sweetheart

Another childhood friend who would figure
prominently in Calvin's later life was schoolgirl
Jayne Centre. The two kids lived across the
Mosholu Parkway from each other. They first
met at PS 80. Both attended the High School of
Industrial Art, and both studied at FIT, where
they finally fell in love. Jayne later became a
textile designer—and Mrs. Calvin Klein.

JACQUES TIFFEAU:
AN ORIGINAL CELEBRITY DESIGNER

Like Calvin Klein, fashion designer Jacques Tiffeau understood the value of understated elegance, creating clothing that grabbed attention because of its cut, shape, and color, not because of frills or fancy design tricks. He adapted materials developed during World War II—double-knits, rayons, plastics, and polyesters—for use in fashion. He was mad for miniskirts, raising hems to new, daring heights. He was one of the first designers to use women of color as models in his fashion shows. He promoted trousers for women at a time when skirts and dresses were the only acceptable attire.

"Tiffeau was avant-garde for his time," said noted American designer James Galanos. "You could put him in the category of the simplicity of Calvin Klein today."

Born in rural France in 1927, Tiffeau started his fashion career as an apprentice tailor before becoming an assistant to legendary French fashion designer Christian Dior. In 1952, he moved to New York City, where he worked as patternmaker and designer for a coat and suit manufacturer before starting up his own company dedicated to creating lower-priced, ready-to-wear apparel for younger women.

This multiple award-winning artist was known for his rise from French peasantry to New York fashion royalty, his rebellion against many of the accepted rules of fashion, and a personal style that could be opinionated, sometimes offensive, and often perceived as outrageous. Jacques Tiffeau died of lung cancer in 1988.

HOW TO TURN A PASSION FOR FASHION INTO A CAREER

So you want to be a fashion designer? Or maybe a fashion illustrator or editor? Perhaps a career in fashion photography is in the cards. Where do you go to learn such things?

Many colleges and universities, as well as trade schools and junior colleges, have programs in fashion design. For a kid with the fashion sense of Calvin Klein, the school of choice was the Fashion Institute of Technology (FIT) in New York City.

Thirteen blocks north, in the heart of the Fashion District, is another of the most celebrated fashion schools in the United States—Parsons The New School for Design. Founded in 1906, this institution boasts such amazing grads as Claire McCardell, Anna Sui, Donna Karan, Marc Jacobs, Alfred Sung, and Tom Ford.

Today, Parsons might be better known as the on-location site where up-and-coming designers vie for the top prize on the TV show *Project Runway*. The program's on-camera mentor, Tim Gunn, was a faculty member at the school for 25 years.

Prominent fashion schools in Canada include Ryerson University, School of Fashion; Kwantlen Polytechnic University; George Brown College— Centre for Fashion Studies and Jewellery; and École Supérieure de Mode de Montréal.

Chapter 3
First Forays into Fashion

As uninspiring as his education at the Fashion Institute of Technology had been, Calvin Klein's first fashion job after graduation was even more mundane. He'd hoped for glamour. What he got was grunt work.

Rising Expectations

At his lackluster workplace, Calvin cut patterns and fabric for $55/week—about two-thirds the average American man's income that year, but in keeping with what a new graduate could expect. "The company ... made dresses out of a fabric it called 'whipped cream,'" said Calvin. "When I went into the shop to cut the first samples at 8:00 a.m., my boss would be

Calvin decided to turn his talents to coats and suits ... it was where the money was.

watching *Captain Kangaroo*." After three months with the lightweight dressmaker, the ambitious young man had had enough. He asked for a raise and, when he was turned down, he quit.

It was at that point that Calvin decided to turn his talents to coats and suits—not necessarily the flashiest sector in the fashion industry, but it was where the money was.

Calvin set his sights on Dan Millstein, Inc., a prominent 7th Avenue company known for turning out top-of-the-line, fur-trimmed coats that sold at the poshest of New York shops. The company also offered made-to-order coats and suits to the city's elite, including opera divas and movie stars, and it had a thriving junior women's line on the side.

Because Millstein—the company—was so respected, it was always overrun with resumes from budding fashion designers like Calvin Klein.

Dan Millstein founded his company in the 1920s, but he truly made his mark during World War II. With a stockpile of fabric at his disposal at a time when it was in short supply, Millstein produced civilian and civil service

A familiar sight in New York: Men transporting racks of clothing on a busy sidewalk in the Garment District. The year is 1955.

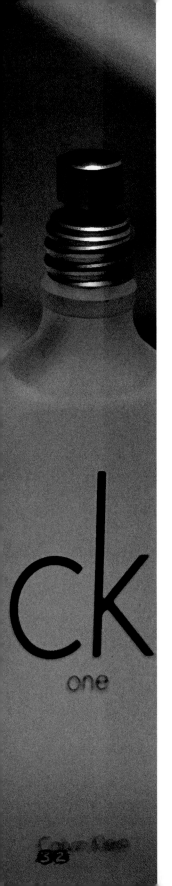

uniforms for the government. After the war, he was among the first Americans to travel to Paris—the soldiers were still in the streets when he arrived. In the war-torn city, he met with such celebrated French designers as Christian Dior and Pierre Cardin, buying their wares and importing the clothing into the United States.

Because Millstein—the company—was so respected, it was always overrun with resumes from budding fashion designers like Calvin Klein. Knowing this, young Cal took a different approach to applying for a job. Instead of going to the owner, Calvin contacted one of the company's star designers, Faye Wagner, a former model whose styles were so popular with the purchasing public that she had her own name line, "Dani Juniors by Faye Wagner." At a time when manufacturer's—not individual designer's—names appeared on labels, Wagner was one of the few who held this honor.

THE FASHION DISTRICT

Today it's as much a funky tourist destination as it is a center for haute couture, but Manhattan's Fashion District (aka the Garment District) hasn't always been so respectable.

In fact, in the late 1800s, it was considered the most corrupt neighborhood in America. Dubbed the "Tenderloin" and the "Devil's Arcade" in those days, the district was the stomping ground for the country's highest concentration of bootleggers, gamblers, and prostitutes. In the early 1900s, the area became a hotbed of hotels, casinos, and rowdy nightlife.

How it transformed from this unruly state to a center of American clothing manufacture is a crazy quilt of circumstances that began in the mid-1800s.

Bounded by 42nd and 34th Streets, 9th Avenue to the west, and Broadway to the east, the Fashion District covers about one square mile (2.6 sq km). Its main thoroughfare, 7th Avenue, is called Fashion Avenue. Many of the buildings constructed during the clothing manufacturing boom of the 1920s are still standing, adding to the district's present-day character. For example, the York Hotel, built in 1920—where Calvin Klein was "discovered"—is still there.

Some former factories are now cool condominiums, showrooms, and shops; a "Needle Threading a Button" sculpture (shown here) marks the location of the Fashion Center Information Kiosk, the first stop for tourists wanting to explore the area; and the Fashion Walk of Fame on Fashion Avenue honors 26 of New York's most influential designers through history.

A Foot in the Door

Calvin got in touch with Wagner and showed her some of his sketches. She was instantly impressed and phoned her boss. "I have a boy down here who showed me a few of his sketches, and they're beautiful," she said. "I'm very interested in him, and I think you should be, too."

Millstein, whose office was furnished with plush furniture, rich carpets, and the work of famous painters, flipped through Calvin's portfolio and saw something he liked. He hired the 19-year-old as a sketcher, a job that paid $75 a week.

As a sketcher, Calvin's job was to translate the ideas in a designer's head onto paper, a tough task for someone as ambitious and opinionated as he was. Still, he and the designer he was assigned to, Maria Prinzi, managed to work well together in the Missy division of Dan Millstein, Inc., for a time.

In those days, Missy was the term for what we now call Plus Size. Calvin, who loved creating looks for long, lean women, had a tough time drawing for the larger figure. On top of that, Millstein was a bit of a bully who criticized and instilled fear into his employees. "He was an impossible man with a colossal temper," said Calvin, who struggled to maintain his enthusiasm for the job.

"I have a boy down here who showed me a few of his sketches, and they're beautiful. I'm very interested in him, and I think you should be, too."

Faye Wagner, designer at Dan Millstein, Inc.

Millstein may have been tough, but he knew his business—a business that could be cut-throat and competitive; a business full of insecurity, jealousy, and greed; a business that demanded strength of character and confidence. Millstein initiated Calvin into this darker side of the industry, toughening him up for the years to come.

Dan Millstein took Calvin to Paris for the first time, introducing him to European designers, runway shows, and haute couture.

Passport to Paris

On the plus side, Dan Millstein took Calvin to Paris for the first time, introducing him to European designers, runway shows, and haute couture. Calvin was enamored with the French sense of flair and took advantage of every spare moment to visit French fashion boutiques and study the style he saw on the streets.

The trips to Paris weren't for pleasure. It was Calvin's job to sketch the outfits Millstein saw on the runway. European designers charged visitors from the United

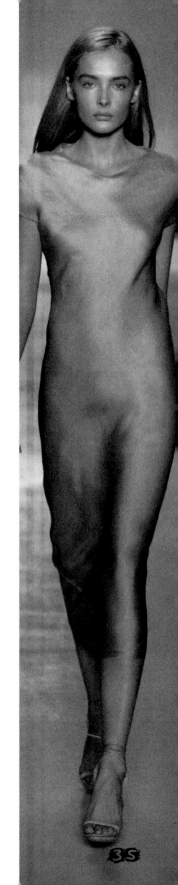

States thousands of dollars admission to their fashion shows because it was common knowledge that American manufacturers came to Paris to view the latest collections and steal ideas. The Americans also had to guarantee they would buy at least two garments from each runway show they attended, an agreement that significantly benefited Mrs. Millstein's wardrobe!

Calvin Klein would sit beside his boss at the side of the runway and, whenever Millstein saw a look he liked, he would nudge his sketcher in the ribs. That was Calvin's signal to commit the outfit to memory, scrutinizing every line and bit of trim. Then, when the show was over, Calvin would dash back to his hotel room and draw what he'd seen. That way, Dan Millstein, Inc., could duplicate—and sell—the same outfit back in New York.

After two years, the thankless job began to wear on Calvin. But, hey, it was a paycheck. To make matters worse, he'd begun to hate the clothes he was forced to sketch. "I needed the job, and had to design those suits but fortunately," he said, "I never saw anyone wear one of them."

Then one day he did. He saw a woman wearing a Millstein outfit he'd helped design. "She was wearing a yellow suit with the yellow fox collar and cuffs, a yellow hat, a yellow handbag, and yellow shoes ... I was sick to think that I had been part of making that outfit possible."

That was when Calvin Klein knew it was time to move on.

Sketches like these are more than just interesting and appealing art. They are an important part of the design process—something that Calvin Klein understood in his early days in the business of fashion design.

Wedding Bells

While the pressure was on Calvin to churn out patterns and sketches in the workplace, the pressure was on him to take the next big step in his personal life, too. His mother, Flo, and girlfriend, Jayne Centre, figured it was time the couple tied the knot.

Although Centre's parents weren't sure about the union—after all, young Cal wasn't making a great wage—the pair wed in the spring of 1964, in a civil ceremony that was followed by a small celebration at the Millstein offices.

Shlansky positioned his young protégée as the next big thing, the one to watch in the fashion biz, a rising star in the Garment District.

A few weeks later, the newlyweds restated their vows in front of friends and family in a spectacular, traditional Jewish wedding ceremony at an elegant hotel overlooking Central Park. At the urging of his wife, Dan Millstein arranged for the couple to have a week-long honeymoon in the Catskill Mountains, in New York state, northwest of New York City.

Immediately after the honeymoon, the young couple moved into a one-bedroom apartment in

In this photo, dated March 1971, Calvin Klein and his wife, Jayne, say goodnight to their daughter, Marci, as they get ready to go out for the evening. As an adult, Marci Klein has had an Emmy Award-winning career as a television producer, most notably for the NBC shows 30 Rock and Saturday Night Live.

Queens to start a life together.

Two years later, Marcia Robin Klein ("Marci"), the couple's only child, was born.

Moving Up and Making a Name

Even though Jayne supplemented her husband's modest salary through her work as a textile designer, the duo struggled to make ends meet—another reason Calvin needed a new, better paying, job.

Despite such high praise and the dash of design freedom he was experiencing, what Calvin longed to do was create his own line.

It wasn't long before he found one at Halldon Ltd., an upscale coat company founded by European refugee Louis Shlansky in 1917. Shlansky was tickled with the idea of stealing Calvin away from Millstein, one of his main competitors, and he knew his well-established firm would benefit from the 21-year-old's energy.

For Calvin, it was a step in the right direction. Halldon, which specialized in faux (false) fur, offered him a four-year contract, a significant salary increase, paid vacations, and a prime design studio space.

At Halldon, unlike his experience at

Millstein, Calvin felt valued. His new employers liked his designs and told him so. They also allowed him a measure of creative freedom within the confines of the genre, price, and style the company was known for.

His early work at Halldon was "inventive and sleek." He worked with tweed, gabardine, and twill, creating coats that sold in the $35 to $45 range. Shlansky positioned his young protégée as the next big thing, the one to watch in the fashion biz, a rising star in the Garment District.

Consequently, Calvin met all the right people, and his magnetic personal charm began to emerge—a shy confidence that endeared him to men and women alike. As the years went by, the name Calvin Klein generated a buzz and it started appearing in the *Tobe Report*—the most significant fashion publication in New York City at the time, a newsletter that highlighted the latest trends, the who's-who, and the where-to-shop.

In April 1967, the Tobe Report hailed Calvin as "one of the more aggressive and imaginative young coat and suit designers." Despite such high praise and the dash of design freedom he was experiencing, what Calvin longed to do was create his own line.

Calvin Klein— the Corporation— Is Born

Calvin was bound by contract not to design clothing on the side while he worked at Halldon Ltd., but he did so anyway. In the evenings and on weekends, he created his own projects at home, teaming up with a patternmaker friend to design a line of coats and dresses.

"I don't know anything about fashion or what you've been studying all these years, but whatever it is, I have a feeling you haven't given it enough of a chance.... I think you'll be miserable if you don't stick it out."

Leo Klein to his son, Calvin

On December 28, 1967, Calvin Klein and Barry Schwartz officially incorporated Calvin Klein Ltd., beginning what would become a 35-year business partnership.

Best Bud Barry

When Barry Schwartz graduated high school at age 16, he was directionless and ended up just hanging around the Mosholu Parkway neighborhood, gambling and visiting the racetrack. Finally, his supermarket-owner father put his foot down and insisted the teenager work with him at the Sundial grocery store.

Barry obliged but, after a few years, he couldn't stand the drudgery of it any more. He wanted something different, so he joined the army. Two months into his basic training, tragedy struck his family. His father was murdered on the job. As the only son, the younger Schwartz was now responsible for supporting the family. He took over the store and quickly boosted business dramatically.

Four years later, on April 4, 1968, and less than three weeks after Barry's wedding day, civil rights leader Martin Luther King Jr. was assassinated. Fueled by anger, frustration, and grief, riots broke out in cities across the United States, including New York City.

In Harlem, the Sundial was trashed, looted, and damaged beyond repair. When Barry saw the irreparable aftermath, he took what he could carry, then tossed the keys into the rubble, never to return to the store. Four days later, he joined Calvin Klein at the York Hotel, and moved from the role of silent partner to hands-on business partner.

When it came time to actually sew the outfits, though, Calvin and his friend figured they'd need about $25,000 for fabric and supplies. They tapped all their Garment District colleagues for a loan, even some friends from Calvin's old Mosholu Parkway days. But money was not to be had.

Calvin was so frustrated, he was ready to give up on his dream, to put fashion aside and start a new career direction. As he sorted through his options, he sat down for a heart-to-heart talk with his longtime pal, Barry Schwartz, who now owned the Schwartz family business, the Sundial grocery store in Harlem.

What Barry suggested to his childhood friend came as a surprise. He said that, if Calvin was serious about giving up on fashion design, he could use him at the supermarket. In fact, he would give his friend half the business, and the two could finally realize their childhood dream of co-owning a grocery store.

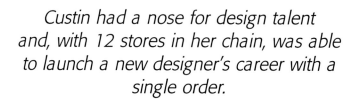

Custin had a nose for design talent and, with 12 stores in her chain, was able to launch a new designer's career with a single order.

Tempted by his friend's offer—but confused and unsure—Calvin turned to his parents for advice, something he rarely did. Again he was surprised by what he heard. What he expected from his father, the former grocery store owner who had never been particularly supportive of his son's career choice, was a push into the supermarket business.

Instead, what he heard was this advice:

"I don't know anything about fashion or what you've been studying all these years, but whatever it is, I have a feeling you haven't given it enough of a chance.... I think you'll be miserable if you don't stick it out."

Armed with his dad's wisdom, Calvin returned to Barry, resolved to stay in the world of design. When he turned down Barry's grocery store offer, his friend surprised him again, this time announcing that he had so much confidence in Calvin's fashion future that he would loan him the money to buy what he needed to get started. Over the coming months, Barry continued to finance the fledgling company with small loans here and there until Calvin insisted the two become business partners.

On December 28, 1967, Calvin Klein and Barry Schwartz officially

incorporated Calvin Klein Ltd., beginning what would become a 35-year business partnership.

Setting Up Shop

The first-ever collection under the Calvin Klein name took three months to put together and consisted of six coats and three dresses.

There was one problem—Calvin's contract with his employer, Halldon Ltd., forbidding him to design on the side, stated that if he did, the garments legally belonged to Halldon. When his boss, Louis Schlansky, found out about Calvin's sideline, he first threatened to take the garments but eventually let the younger man—and his clothes—go without a fight.

A few days later, in March 1968, Calvin set up a makeshift showroom in Room 613 of the York Hotel, a venue used by designers and garment sellers to show their wares to prospective clients. Most buyers made appointments to see collections of interest, but they would also drop in unannounced to see the work of up-and-coming designers.

Room 613 was perfectly situated across from the elevator doors—anyone stepping off the elevator could see right into Calvin's tiny showroom.

For weeks, Calvin sat in his room working the phone, calling buyers and fashion writers trying to convince them to come see his collection. He got a few orders this way, but not enough to pay the rent.

Then one day, the elevator doors accidentally opened on the sixth floor of the York Hotel, and an executive from Bonwit Teller—an upscale

FASHION FINDS

Calvin Klein wasn't the first young designer whose career was helped along by Bonwit Teller president Mildred Custin. By the time Calvin came along, she had already introduced three European designers to the American market:

- Italian-born French designer Pierre Cardin created brightly colored, chunky, geometric fashions for women in the 1950s and 1960s. He is also the creator of the signature high-buttoned, collarless jackets worn by the Beatles.

- French designer André Courrèges, best known for his space-age creations in the 1960s, is credited with inventing the mini-skirt.

- The work of French-born Italian designer Emanuel Ungaro, who worked with Courrèges in the 1960s, merges contrasting colors, mixes bold patterns, and celebrates femininity.

BONWIT TELLER & CO.
The Specialty Shop of Originations
Fifth Avenue at 38th Street, New York

Bathing Apparel & Accessories

When Calvin Klein made his first big sale to Bonwit Teller, he became a part of one of the oldest, most respected clothing establishments in the nation Shown here: a Bonwit Teller advertisement for "bathing apparel" in 1916.

5th Avenue department store—got a glimpse of the Calvin Klein collection.

The visitor, Don O'Brien, was on his way to another appointment on a higher floor and continued as planned but, after his scheduled meeting, he returned to the sixth floor—this time on purpose. He wanted a closer look at the garments he'd seen from the elevator door.

O'Brien liked what he saw on the racks in Room 613 and invited Calvin to show his collection to Bonwit Teller president Mildred Custin a few days later.

Known as the *grande dame* in the fashion industry of the day, Custin had a nose for design talent and, with 12 stores in her chain, was able to launch a new designer's career with a single order. "If I saw something I liked, I'd fill the store with it," she said. "I trusted my judgment."

The following Saturday, Calvin rolled his rack of clothing 20 blocks to Bonwit Teller. "I didn't want to pile the clothes into a taxi and crease anything," he said. "Getting the clothes to Bonwit's was a nightmare because one of the wheels broke."

When Calvin arrived, he presented his dresses and coats to Custin. She approved of what she saw and placed an order for $50,000 worth of garments on the spot. "What impressed me most was the purity of his line and the simplicity of his designs," said Custin later.

The sale was more than the 25-year-old designer expected to make in his first year, let alone on his first order.

FASHION IN THE CITY—
A HISTORY OF
NEW YORK COUTURE

New York City has been the hub of the U.S. fashion biz since the 1860s—the Civil War years. At the time, NYC was home to the nation's largest textile storage facilities, so when the military needed thousands of uniforms for its soldiers, the government turned to the manufacturers who already had the fabric at hand.

The New York garment industry boomed. By the end of the 1860s, when most Americans were buying ready-made clothes rather than sewing their own, New York had become the hub of U.S. clothing manufacturing.

During this same time, one particular district in New York City was becoming home to thousands of immigrants who had moved in to work in the booming business. The lofts where they worked started pushing boundaries, moving into the more upscale parts of town, something the city's upper-crust citizens didn't like.

They didn't want to mingle with people they considered "riff raff," so they convinced the city to create a zoning bylaw that confined clothing factories—and therefore the immigrant workers—to the quadrant now known as the Garment District.

Today, most clothing construction is done overseas, where labor is non-unionized and, therefore, cheaper. But this little piece of Manhattan is where the U.S. fashion industry still lives—and generates billions of dollars every year. Trends are set here, thousands of people still work here, and major design houses, including Calvin Klein, Inc., are still headquartered here.

These buildings on 40th Street, between 6th and 7th avenues, look down on Bryant Park in the heart of the Fashion District.

Chapter 4
The '70s and '80s— The Rising Star

Now that Calvin Klein and Barry Schwartz had their first order—and such a big order—it was time for them to get to work. Because the two young men were the only employees of the newly formed company, Calvin Klein Ltd., it meant they had to do it all.

A Two-Man Show

"We did everything," said Barry. "We pressed coats. We shipped the coats. We swept the floor. There were nights when we would iron and pack until the early hours."

They often slept at the office. Their moms even helped where they could, hand-sewing labels into the coats and dresses. "It was seven

After a grueling production period, they made their deadline—Bonwit Teller got its full order, on time, as promised.

days a week in the shop, often 24 hours a day," said Calvin.

After a grueling production period, they made their deadline—Bonwit Teller got its full order, on time, as promised, and once the clothes were on the racks at the store, women snapped them up. Before long, other department stores, in other states, came calling. They, too, wanted to sell Calvin Klein garments.

Moving Fashion Forward

As the word started to get out about this hot new designer, Bonwit Teller president Mildred Custin had even bigger plans for him. Up to that point, the fashions at her department store had been geared to the wealthy, middle-aged market. Now Custin wanted to reach out to younger, hipper women who likely had less money to spend but who wanted nice outfits. So, in September 1968, she set aside the store's eighth floor to showcase fashions geared to that group. She chose Calvin Klein's fall collection as the one to kick off her new concept.

...all eight of the store's 5th Avenue picture windows featured a single mannequin, each wearing a Klein original...

Calvin Klein works with a model as he creates his Spring 1975 line. Klein's business partner Barry Schwartz looks on. The boards behind them are covered with fabric swatches and clothing sketches.

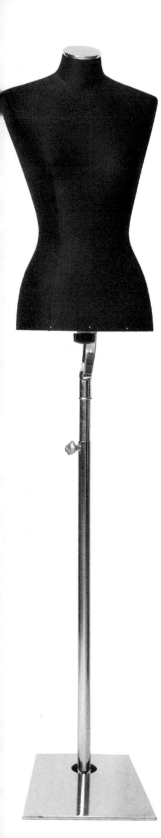

To promote the new eighth floor "Miss Bonwit Shop," Custin broke another store rule. Until then, only the best-known designers had the privilege of having their work displayed in Bonwit Teller's street-level windows. Calvin would become the first newcomer to merit that honor, and he wouldn't just have one window dedicated to his designs—which would have been amazing enough for an unknown like him. Instead, all eight of the store's 5th Avenue picture windows featured a single mannequin, each wearing a Klein original, and each with a little sign that read "Calvin Klein, Miss Bonwit Shop, Eighth Floor."

The day after the window displays went in, excited buyers rushed into the store to snap up Calvin's trendy dresses and coats. To make things even better, Bonwit Teller took out a full-page ad on page five of the Sunday *New York Times* to promote Calvin's new collection, something they did at least once a month for the next year. "Whatever was shown on page five of the *Times* on Sunday, you could expect buyers from other stores to be in the showroom on Monday morning," said the store's vice-president of sales. "If a Bonwit Teller advertisement appeared, the merchandise sold."

That's exactly what happened in this case. Suddenly, Calvin Klein Ltd. had orders from Philadelphia, San Francisco, and Washington, D.C., along with other high-end New York City stores like Saks Fifth Avenue and Bergdorf Goodman. By the end of its first fall season, the new company had earned $500,000. By the end of the first year, sales had reached $1 million.

Sprinting into the '70s

With the success of their first year in business, Calvin and Barry moved into bigger headquarters in the heart of New York's Fashion District—into a building that still houses the company showrooms today.

Calvin was the visionary—he came up with the clothing concepts. Barry had the business sense to turn those visions into reality.

In this new location, they could do all their work—business and production—in one place. They also hired new staff—a sales associate, three young design assistants, and a publicist.

As the business boomed, Calvin knew he needed a healthy relationship with the fashion press, and it was the publicist's job to help make this happen. With her help, Calvin connected with an editor at *Harper's Bazaar*, who presented his clothing in almost every issue for the next three years. He was featured on the cover of *Vogue* magazine in 1969. A year later, he showed his collection on a daytime TV program called *Dinah's Place*, hosted by legendary talk-show host Dinah Shore. He also participated in charity fashion shows and promoted himself at home in New York City by visiting Bonwit Teller's eighth floor and personally helping women choose their outfits.

Calvin's boyish good looks and boy-next-door nature, combined with his winning sense of style, made him a favorite of the fashion elite—who took him to all the right parties—and a pet subject of the fashion press—who put him on their pages.

A Perfect Partnership

While Calvin Klein loved the media attention, meeting new people, and being in the limelight, his partner, Barry Schwartz, preferred to stay in the background. It was one of the reasons their partnership worked so well for so long. "It was the ideal partnership because we didn't compete," said Barry.

Calvin was the visionary—he came up with the clothing concepts. Barry had the business sense to turn those visions into reality. The charismatic Calvin created the company's image, while Barry did the financial dealings. "I always believed in him," said Barry, "but it was pretty easy to believe in him, because he's a pretty impressive guy."

Together, this pair created a fashion empire that made them rich by the time they were 30. Each collection was more successful than the one before it—but that didn't mean the designer was ready to put his feet up and take it easy.

In 1973, he decided it was time to branch out from coats and dresses, and expand into a whole new fashion line of women's sportswear. That year, he created a 74-piece collection, and the simple, spare, sleek "Calvin Klein Look" was born.

That year, Calvin Klein became a full-fledged superstar in the fashion world. His new collection, and its modern take on fashion, earned him his first Coty Award, the highest honor in American fashion at the time. He was the youngest person ever to win the award and the first person to win it three years in a row.

If Calvin was a brilliant designer, he also had a genius sense of timing and a knack for knowing what the fashion-wearing public wanted. While the concept of luxury sportswear—comfortable, fashionable clothing made from the finest fabrics—was becoming big in Europe, it hadn't yet reached North America. Calvin was one of the first to bring designer fashion to the mainstream in the United States. Said Jeffrey Banks, one of Calvin's early assistants:

"The thing about Calvin is that he has this sixth sense for knowing what people want before they know they want it."

IMPRESSING THE FASHION PRESS

Until the 1960s, most fashion designers weren't known by name. They worked quietly in their workshops making garments under a manufacturer's label or store name. By the mid-1960s, that began to change. Women started to become interested in the people who actually created the fashions they wore. This was partly thanks to First Lady Jacqueline Kennedy, her interest in fashion, and the fact that she talked up the designers who made her outfits. (Oleg Cassini, Christian Dior, Coco Chanel, and Hubert de Givenchy were her faves.)

Because of this rising interest in designers, society columnists started writing about which celebrities were wearing which designers' fashions, and the prominent magazine *Women's Wear Daily* began promoting designers, their clothing, and the people who wore them. Suddenly, the trade papers could make or break a designer's career.

Thus began the days of fashion designers as superstars—Calvin Klein was one of the first, and certainly has been one of the most celebrated. Now, of course, every celebrity on the red carpet is asked, "Who are you wearing?"

An Oscar for Best Dress Goes to ...

The elegant, floor-length gown Calvin Klein created for actress Gwyneth Paltrow (right) for the 1996 Academy Awards is regularly named as one of the Best Oscar Dresses of All Times. "A love of sensual simplicity brought me and Gwyneth together on this dress," said Calvin. "She understands that restraint is a part of great style. She showed up alone and went through the fabric bolts with me and chose the pink Charmeuse. Two fittings and we were done."

Other celebs who love their Calvins are Eva Mendes, Renée Zellweger, Hilary Swank, Julia Roberts, Helen Hunt, Sandra Bullock, and Bianca Jagger.

Gwyneth Paltrow in her Calvin Klein original at the 1996 Oscars.

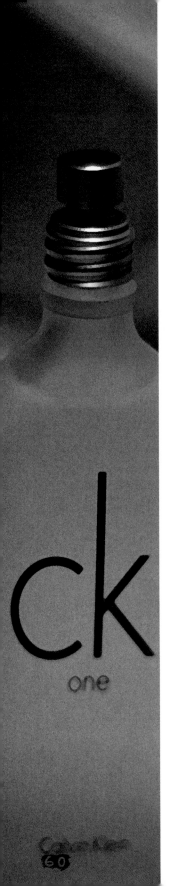

Making a Name

It was Banks who first put the Calvin Klein name on the outside of a garment. Without meaning to, he launched the logo-wear trend that is still hot today.

As a thank-you to his new boss for hiring him, Banks had a special T-shirt made in Calvin's favorite color—chocolate brown. Then he had the Calvin Klein logo printed onto the shirt's sleeve. When Banks presented the shirt to his mentor, Calvin admired it, then put it aside, not giving it a second thought. A few weeks later, Barry Schwartz happened to spot the T-shirt tossed in with other things on the shelves in Calvin's office.

Calvin was one of the first to bring designer fashion to the mainstream in the United States.

Barry asked his partner if the brown T-shirt was part of the line that was about to be presented in a runway show. "No," said Calvin. "Who'd want to wear my name?"

Then young Banks had another brainstorm. He ordered a selection of T-shirts in a rainbow of colors to match the shades of the outfits to be seen in the upcoming fashion show, and he had the Calvin Klein logo printed onto the sleeve of each T-shirt, just as he'd done with the chocolate brown one.

At the fashion show, staff members wore the shirts, and by the next day, "everybody wanted the T-shirt that said Calvin Klein," said Banks.

Leader of the Brand

In the mid-1970s, Calvin and Barry discovered the value of licensing the Calvin Klein name to other companies, a strategy that is common today but was just getting going back then.

The first licensing deal for Calvin Klein was with a fur coat manufacturer called Alixandre. It made sense that, if a woman bought a Calvin Klein evening outfit, she might also like a Calvin Klein fur to go with it. The strategy worked, earning income for the young businessmen and helping Alixandre sell more coats.

By the end of the decade, the Calvin Klein name was on belts, umbrellas, shoes, scarves, sunglasses, and sewing patterns—all made by other companies.

THE ACADEMY AWARDS OF FASHION

The Coty American Fashion Critics' Awards, once considered the Oscars of American fashion design, were created by perfume company Coty, Inc., to celebrate excellence in the American fashion industry.

First presented in 1943, the awards were discontinued in 1985. By then, the Council of Fashion Designers of America (CFDA) Fashion Awards were in full swing. Founded in 1962, the CFDA handed out its first annual Fashion Awards in 1981. Every June since then, the who's-who in American fashion have gathered to celebrate the best in the biz. Calvin Klein has won six Coty Awards and six CFDA Awards.

The company's two founders, still in their 30s, were millionaires.

The biggest—and most valuable—licensing deals the duo negotiated during their careers began in the late 1970s and early 1980s. They came in the forms of cosmetics, menswear and, of course, the famous Calvin Klein jeans.

Business Boomed, Family Faltered

With Calvin's star on the rise, and his work life becoming busier and busier, he had less and less time for his wife, Jayne, and daughter, Marci. His marriage was in trouble. "We grew in different directions," said Calvin.

By the time Marci was six, the family home was in Queens, but her hard-working dad spent many nights in the city, often sleeping at his office. In August 1974, her parents divorced.

After the marriage ended, Calvin got involved in the downtown nightlife and club scene. Studio 54 was the place to hang out when it opened in 1977. Artists, singers, actors, other designers, models—everyone who was anyone danced the night away at the legendary, world-famous disco.

Studio 54 was also the place where one of the best offers of his career came to Calvin.

"If you were around a hundred years from now and wanted a definitive picture of the American look in 1975, you'd study Calvin Klein."

Vogue magazine, September 1975

PRICE YOUR NAME

Branding products with designer names has become big business and a significant source of income for the designers. It's called licensing.

What happens is this: The owner of the name allows another company to make a product with that name on it. Say an umbrella company wants to make a Calvin Klein umbrella. If Calvin likes the umbrella, consents to have his name on it, and lets the company sell it, the company pays him a royalty, or a set amount of money, for each umbrella sold. The brand name helps the company sell more products, and the person with the name earns more money.

One night, a stranger approached him on the dance floor and said, "How would you like to put your name on jeans?" At the time, designer jeans had barely begun to hit the stores, and only one designer, Gloria Vanderbilt, was really making them work.

"I always liked the idea that I would be able to reach more people. That's why the jeans interested me," said Calvin. "The jeans gave me the opportunity to get the message across to the masses."

Calvin was heading to Germany the next morning, so he left the matter in his business partner's hands. By the time Calvin returned to the United States, Barry had negotiated a fantastic deal with Puritan Fashions, the company that would make the jeans. This deal, in fact, is legendary in the fashion world as one of the smartest licensing arrangements of all time.

In addition to a million-dollar signing bonus, Puritan agreed to give $1 to Calvin Klein Ltd. for every pair of Calvin Klein jeans sold. When the jeans with the Calvin Klein label on the back pocket went on the market in 1978, more than 200,000 pairs sold in the first week. With their newfound wealth, Calvin and Barry bought shares in Puritan Fashions and a few years later bought the entire company as part of Calvin Klein, Inc.

Brooke's Backside

By 1980, all kinds of big names were getting into the designer jeans business. To stay ahead of the competition, Calvin Klein teamed up with top fashion photographer Richard Avedon

and created some of the most controversial television ads in history.

The most famous of those commercials featured 15-year-old model Brooke Shields wearing tight Calvin Klein jeans and a loose shirt. She looked into the camera and asked: "You want to know what comes between me and my Calvins? Nothing."

The reaction to the ads was instant and overwhelming. Some people objected to the ads because Brooke was so young, and her image and words were so adult. Other people recognized that the ads would change the future of fashion advertising.

Despite the difference in public opinion, the ads did what they were supposed to do. They sold jeans. More than 400,000 pairs of jeans flew off the shelves the week after the TV spot first aired in 1980. Over the next while, the company sold two million pairs of Calvin Klein jeans a month, earning $12.5 million in royalties that first year.

DID YOU KNOW?

The first time Calvin Klein tried to launch designer jeans, they flopped. They didn't fit well and, at $50 a pair, they were more expensive than Gloria Vanderbilt jeans, the only other designer name-brand jeans on the market. That was in 1976. Two years later, Calvin Klein's redesigned, well-made jeans would sell like hotcakes!

Two years later, the radical television commercials—and related magazine ads—were still such a hot topic of discussion that Brooke and Calvin appeared together on the cover of *People* magazine, illustrating an article about how the commercials "made Calvin the best-known name in U.S. fashion." This was the first of many brazen Calvin Klein advertising campaigns that would serve to keep his name in the news and his clothing front-and-center in shoppers' minds.

Menswear and Underwear

As early as 1975, Calvin dreamed of moving into menswear. He believed it would be simple to re-interpret his women's wear designs as men's clothing because they were natural and muted. "He wanted to have men's because he thought it would make the [fashion] shows more dramatic," said design assistant Jeffrey Banks.

It took three years but, in 1978, Calvin Klein licensed the first menswear collection—suits, coats, pants, shirts, sweaters, accessories, and, most noteworthy, underwear. Until then, men didn't think much about their underclothes. It was usually mothers and wives who bought the necessary unmentionables.

Calvin saw an opportunity to change that and, in 1982—at the height of the Calvin Klein designer jeans craze—he launched a line of men's briefs, boxers, bikinis, and T-shirts at Bloomingdale's. Even though they were almost twice the price of other underwear, they were an instant hit, selling 400 dozen pieces within five days.

Calvin Klein and Brooke Shields are shown with Steve Rubell, co-owner of the celebrated New York disco Studio 54. When this photo was taken in 1981, Rubell had recently been released from prison, where he and his business partner had served time after being convicted of tax evasion.

Calvin Klein leads his daughter, Marci, away from a building on 97th Street in New York after she was released by kidnappers who had held her for ransom.

THE WORST DAY OF CALVIN KLEIN'S LIFE

One morning in March 1978, 11-year-old Marci Klein was on her way to school, when a former babysitter stopped her and tricked her into thinking her dad was sick and needed her help. Marci went with the babysitter, who turned out to be a kidnapper. She and her two partners-in-crime took Marci to an apartment, where they held her for $100,000 in ransom.

To save his daughter, Calvin Klein called police, then got the money and dropped it off, as directed by the kidnappers, who then told him where to find Marci. The worried dad found the building easily but he couldn't find the exact apartment where Marci was held. "All of a sudden I hear him screaming my name," said Marci, years later. "I hear him banging, banging, banging on all these doors." The little girl called out to her dad so he could find her.

Before the ordeal was over, the FBI mistook Calvin for one of the kidnappers but quickly realized their mistake. It wasn't long before the real kidnappers were captured and jailed. "That was a nightmare that changed our lives a great deal," said Calvin, who then understood all too clearly the dangers of being a wealthy celebrity.

Suddenly men were interested in underwear. Another daring poster campaign further pushed sales and, every year, Calvin added new colors—purple, blue, oatmeal, red—to keep the guys coming back season after season.

Next, he tackled women's undies, coming up with a line that included boxer shorts and briefs inspired by men's boxers and briefs. Again came a radical ad campaign and, again, sales were beyond anyone's wildest expectations—$70 million in one year.

The Scent of Success

By the mid-1980s, one product Calvin didn't have, and one he wanted, was a signature fragrance. Other designers were leading the way on that front, and Calvin wanted to be part of the trend. After one failed attempt at creating a fragrance in 1977, Calvin and partner Barry Schwartz linked up with a beauty product manufacturer to get the perfume side of the business going.

Together, Calvin, Barry, and the beauty product manufacturer created Obsession and, once again, Calvin had a hit on his hands, helped along by yet another provocative advertising campaign. Within months of its release, Obsession had earned multi-millions of dollars for the company. Obsession lotion, soap, and bath products soon followed, with Obsession for Men making its debut a year later.

By the end of the 1980s, stores carried four different Calvin Klein fragrances after Eternity and Eternity for Men joined the parade of products. Since then, 30 more perfumes have been added to the collection.

CALVIN KLEIN IN THE MOVIES—1985

Calvin Klein underwear has become such an iconic part of American fashion that it was featured in a classic moment in the 1985 Hollywood movie *Back to the Future*. In this scene, teenage time traveler Marty McFly (Michael J. Fox) goes back 30 years and meets his future mother Lorraine (Lea Thompson):

Lorraine: "I've never seen red underwear before, Calvin."

Marty: "Calvin? Why do you keep calling me Calvin?"

Lorraine: "Well, that's your name isn't it—Calvin Klein? It's written all over your underwear."

The Personal and Professional Meet

At the same time that Calvin's business life was soaring, his personal life was again on a similar course. In 1981, he'd hired a 21-year-old design assistant named Kelly Rector. The daughter of a fashion model and TV director, Kelly had grown up in the lap of luxury in Westport, Connecticut, until her parents divorced.

When her mom remarried and moved Kelly and her sister to New York City, Kelly fell in love with the fashion world. She attended the Fashion Institute of Technology—as had Calvin—and started working for Klein competitor Ralph Lauren soon after. (She had actually applied and been interviewed for a job at Calvin Klein in the past but hadn't been hired.)

One night, when Kelly was out dancing, she ran into Calvin at Studio 54. The next morning, he called her and offered her a job. She jumped at the chance to work as an assistant to the star designer. Before long, Kelly was promoted from design assistant to design director. By then, she had also become Calvin's muse—the person who inspired his creative work—and his best friend.

In 1986, during a fabric-buying trip to Italy, Kelly became Calvin's wife. "We decided to get married in Rome because we both love Italy so much," said Calvin of the spur-of-the-moment marriage. "We were here for work and decided to marry before going back to New York."

For the wedding, the bride wore an off-white silk suit designed by who else but Calvin Klein? The following day, the newlyweds got right back to the business of shopping for fine fabrics.

The new marriage signaled the beginning of a quieter period in Calvin's world—he slowed down a bit and lived a somewhat lower-profile lifestyle with his new love. Kelly Klein soon took a new job with *House & Garden* magazine but was still there for her husband when he needed her—and he would soon need her love and support more than ever.

Despite the success of Calvin Klein jeans, Calvin Klein fragrances, Calvin Klein underwear, and Calvin Klein men's and women's wear, things were not perfect at the house of Klein. By the end of the 1980s, Calvin was struggling with personal demons, and his company was struggling financially.

Kelly and Calvin Klein are photographed at a gala event at New York's Metropolitan Museum of Art.

Chapter 5
The 1990s—
The Fall and Rise
of Calvin Klein

In the 1980s, fashion was big—literally. At work, women wore "power suits" with huge shoulder pads to make them look bigger and more powerful as they moved into what was, at that time, still largely a man's world. Many hairstyles were looking big, too, and hairsprayed to the max, to hold their shape all day. The stars of the TV show *Dynasty* (1981–1989) embodied the dress of the day.

A Time for Bigger and Better

Workout videos made their debut in the early 1980s, with the *Jane Fonda Workout* becoming the top-selling workout video of all time.

Despite Barry's efforts, Calvin Klein, Inc.—or CKI, as the business was now called—was struggling as it moved into the next decade.

Suddenly—at least for those who could afford to spend the money and the time—fit was fashionable and, by the late 1980s, it showed on the fashion runways. Mere models were out; "supermodels"—tall, athletic, and imposing—were in. And they were wealthy. Linda Evangelista once famously said, "We don't wake up for less than $10,000 a day."

After Ronald Reagan was elected U.S. president in 1980, the decade became one in which people were encouraged to make their own way in the world and to rely less on the government for support. It was an era when people who had money made more money, thanks to the politics and social structure of the time. More people had more disposable income. This meant they were making enough money after taxes and paying for necessities to save or spend on such things as the newly invented home computer, air travel, and designer clothing.

Living the High Life

As this decade of excess progressed, Calvin became wealthier and more famous. He was at the top of his game, earning three Council of Fashion Designers of America (CFDA) Fashion Awards (1982, 1983, and 1986). He was the first fashion designer to live the extravagant life of a movie star, attending posh parties and hanging out with the most glamorous people. The paparazzi loved him and followed his every move.

His lavish lifestyle eventually caught up with him, though and, in May 1988, when he was supposed to be on a nationwide tour to

British supermodel Yasmin Le Bon is shown in 1989 modeling a gold, strapless satin silk dress by Calvin Klein. Tall, imposing, and super-fit, Le Bon exemplified the 1980s fashion-design "look."

promote his new fragrance, Eternity, he strangely vanished from the public eye.

Given Calvin's celebrity status, he couldn't hide from the media for long. After a few weeks, he came clean and let the world know where he was—he had checked into a rehab center for alcohol and prescription drug abuse.

Later, he explained that it was his lack of life experience, combined with the excesses of his whirlwind existence, that had led him astray. He hadn't realized how damaging his behavior and bad habits had become until it was too late. "I learned the hard way, and I paid the price," he said. "It was all new. I just didn't know any better."

By his side as he recovered from his addictions were wife Kelly and partner Barry Schwartz. Barry kept the business going while his friend healed.

Tough Times

Despite Barry's efforts, Calvin Klein, Inc.—or CKI, as the business was now called—was struggling as it moved into the next decade. During the larger-than-life 1980s, the company had taken on a huge debt, believing the money would continue to flow in. It didn't.

The bottom had fallen out of the designer jeans market. Since 1985, people just weren't buying jeans the way they used to. A conflict over the menswear line led to a lawsuit and halted sales of the men's collections for a few years. CKI was also fighting with the maker of its fragrances. To top things off, the United States was stuck in a recession that had started when the stock market crashed in 1987.

That meant shoppers weren't spending the way they used to.

All these things added up to tough times for Klein and company. By 1992, CKI had no cash and no way to rebuild its bank account. In fact, Klein and Schwartz were just about to declare bankruptcy when Calvin's good friend, record producer David Geffen, stepped in and saved the day. He paid the company's $62 million debt and told Klein and Schwartz to pay him back whenever they could—no strings attached. "David didn't get anything out of it," said a grateful Barry Schwartz. "David did it as a friend."

He paid the company's $62 million debt and told Klein and Schwartz to pay him back whenever they could—no strings attached.

The Reinvention of Calvin Klein

Before long, the company started to turn around. Calvin Klein and Barry Schwartz took an honest look at all aspects of the business. They asked themselves what worked, what didn't, what they wanted to change, and how they wanted to sell their products.

They completely restructured the company.

They opened a series of Calvin Klein boutiques that only sold Calvin Klein clothing and accessories. They teamed up with an Italian manufacturer to re-launch their menswear collection, which was an instant success. Jeans eventually started to make a comeback, so they also got back into the denim business, this time with different types of jeans, shirts, skirts, dresses, and jackets.

Within a year, the partners had repaid the money they owed David Geffen. The company had weathered a rough patch and was moving in a healthy direction once again. Rather than taking it easy, though, Calvin knew it was time to take another big step forward and launch a new line.

With cK, Calvin had another success on his hands. Calvin Klein, the company, was back on track...

The trouble was, he didn't have a clear concept of what the new line would be—until his daughter had something to say about it. A recent college grad, then in her 20s, Marci Klein told her father she couldn't afford to wear his clothes and, even if she could, they just weren't her style. "It's simply not appropriate for me to be spending that kind of money or

CALVIN KLEIN IN THE MOVIES—1995

In the 1995 movie *Clueless*, actress Alicia Silverstone played a sweet society teen named Cher. In this scene, Cher is dressed for a date in a see-through blouse over a revealing white slip dress. Her dad, Mel, played by Dan Hedaya, is shocked at his daughter's outfit.

Mel: "What is that?"

Cher: "It's a dress."

Mel: "Says who?"

Cher: "Calvin Klein!"

dressing that way," she said one evening at dinner. "There are so many people like me. Why don't you make clothes for us?"

The "people like me" Marci was talking about were the young adults of Generation X, born between 1964 and 1981. Her comments inspired her designer dad, who soon came up with a younger, hipper, less expensive line geared to Marci's age group. In 1993, Calvin launched the line, called simply cK, with a fashion show featuring "real people" instead of models—people with dreadlocks, tattoos, and piercings.

With cK, Calvin had another success on his hands. Calvin Klein, the company, was back on track, as was Calvin Klein, the man. That same year, Calvin was named America's Best Designer.

Controversy over Kate and Marketing with Marky Mark

At the same time Calvin Klein was reinventing himself and his business, he was, as always, stirring up controversy in the way he promoted his fashions and fragrances.

By the early 1990s, the "bigger is better" way of thinking was over. The new phrase of the day was "kinder and gentler," a concept that played out in North American fashion and day-to-day life.

On the runways and in advertising, designers moved away from the towering, super-fit supermodels of the 1980s, choosing instead to show their clothes on smaller, more fragile women. Calvin Klein's muse during this

Calvin Klein's Rivals—The Other All-Americans

Like Calvin Klein, Tommy Hilfiger and Ralph Lauren are considered all-American boys in the design world, specializing in comfortable, fuss-free fashions for mainstream North America. All three are from New York—Klein and Lauren from the same neighborhood in the Bronx, and Hilfiger from upstate. Each designer shares in common the fact that they are international superstars, publicity wizards, and brand names. The designs of all three are seen on the runways of the world's fashion centers, as well as in mainstream department stores.

Ralph Lauren, who was born Ralph Lifshitz, is a few years older than Klein. He started out making ties and is now renowned for his classy—and classic—men's and women's wear. His Polo brand is recognized around the world.

The style of Tommy Hilfiger, who is about eight years younger than Klein, is possibly the most street-savvy of the trio. Like Lauren, this father of four has no formal design training, just a sense of what real people want.

If there's a fourth all-American in this group, it is Donna Karan (born Donna Faske). Also from New York City, Karan creates women's clothing she would wear herself. Her simple, comfortable, feminine business attire is designed for real women's curves. Her DKNY line offers younger, hipper, and less expensive options.

Above and opposite: Models walk the runway at the Tommy Hilfiger Collection for Fall/Winter 2010 during Fashion Week on February 18, 2010, in New York.

period was English model Kate Moss, a gamine girl who had been discovered by a modeling agent in an airport at age 14. Four years later, Calvin chose her as the face of a new ad campaign for his Obsession fragrance—and stirred up another controversy.

Moss was criticized for her extreme thinness, and Calvin Klein was criticized for promoting the boyish look as beautiful.

Kate Moss looked like a skinny schoolgirl—the exact opposite of the tall, curvy models of the previous decade. Moss was criticized for her extreme thinness, and Calvin Klein was criticized for promoting the boyish look as beautiful.

Calvin Klein didn't just advertise to girls and women. He also had men's clothing and underwear to think about, so once again, he made a bold advertising statement. This time, he brought in young, handsome rapper Mark Wahlberg, better known as "Marky Mark," one of the original members of the boy-band New Kids on the Block.

In the early 1990s, Marky had a solo career and a number one hit with his rap-dance song "Good Vibrations." He was a fit 20-year-old with a following. He was also known for wearing low-slung jeans that showed off the elastic

Kate Moss models an outfit from the new cK line for younger women on April 10, 1994, in New York City. In a departure from the larger, more fit and athletic look of many models in the 1980s, the 1990s featured models who, like Moss, seemed more fragile or even boyish in their appearance. Not everyone felt that such a "thin" look was necessarily a healthy or natural one for young women and girls to imitate.

band of his underwear—a perfect place to show off the Calvin Klein name on briefs and boxers.

"Marky's involvement was such a natural progression for me," said the designer. "He is the quintessential symbol of the young hip crowd to whom the clothing appeals."

The rapper, who has since gone on to become a famous film actor and producer, appeared in his Calvins—and nothing but his Calvins—in television commercials and on a giant billboard in New York City's Times Square. The advertising campaign helped Mark Wahlberg become a Hollywood star—and helped Calvin Klein sell millions of dollars worth of underwear.

The Ads Go Too Far

It is said that "there is no such thing as bad publicity"—a statement that is mostly true in Calvin Klein's case. No matter how radical his advertising, it always served to keep his name in the public eye.

In 1995, though, Calvin Klein went too far. That year, a series of ads for cK jeans featured partially naked teenagers. The advertisements ran in teen magazines, on billboards, on buses, and on television. The public was outraged. The kids in the photos were too young, critics said. They weren't professional models, and were portrayed in a way that many felt was too adult. CKI defended the artistry of the ads for three weeks, but when the public protest showed no signs of stopping, the company canceled the campaign.

It was too late. Calvin Klein's reputation had been damaged. *Forbes* magazine called the ad campaign the worst of the year. The FBI and

TOO SKINNY?

Some models, just like some women, are naturally thin. Twiggy, a fashion icon of the 1960s, was discovered at a hair salon at age 16, and quickly became "the face of '66." A year later, she was an international modeling superstar known for her big eyes, boyish haircuts, and stick-thin figure. Thirty years later, along came Kate Moss, another woman who comes by her waif-like look honestly.

For most women, this look isn't natural, and nor is it healthy. Yet many girls and women can't resist the thin-is-in theory. They go to dangerous extremes of diet and exercise, trying to lose weight to match what they think is a glamorous movie star or model look.

The fashion industry continues to be heavily criticized for promoting bony bodies as beautiful. Fortunately, a campaign to promote healthy bodies is taking hold, and girls and women are learning that whatever their natural body type is, that is what's best for them.

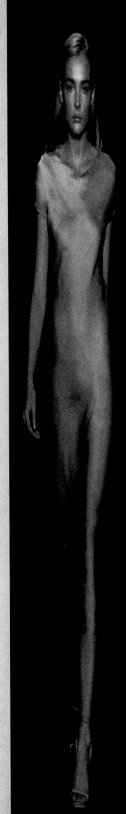

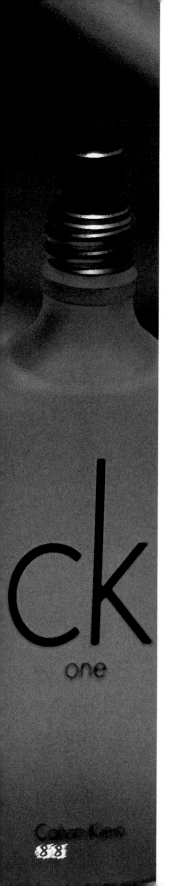

the U.S. Justice Department launched an investigation. U.S. President Bill Clinton called the ads "outrageous," and First Lady Hillary Clinton said it was "exploitation of children." In 2003, the trade magazine *Adweek* listed the cK campaign as one of "the most offensive, most tasteless and downright dumbest ads of the last decade."

In 2003, the trade magazine Adweek *listed the cK campaign as one of "the most offensive, most tasteless and downright dumbest ads of the last decade."*

A year after that ad campaign was pulled, Calvin Klein suffered another advertising misstep. This time it was a campaign to promote his new fragrance, cK be, and this time, he used young models so skinny and grungy, they were said to look like destitute street kids. Criticized for glamorizing a culture that revolves around drug use, Calvin said the ads were designed to be "real" in a time when most advertisements were airbrushed and phony. Again the public protested and, again, President Clinton voiced his disapproval.

With 1999 came another disastrous series of ads—this time for the launch of Calvin Klein underwear for kids. This set of images showed children under age six wearing nothing but underpants. Again Calvin was criticized, and again he was forced to remove the advertising.

The Ups and Downs of a Decade

It's true he made some mistakes along the way, but there was much good news for Calvin Klein in the 1990s. It was during this decade that he launched a home décor collection called Calvin Klein Home, and he licensed his name to a number of other product lines, including sleepwear, swimwear, and purses. He opened his flagship store on Madison Avenue, near Central Park in New York City, and half a dozen stores in Europe, Asia, and the Middle East. He earned three more CFDA Fashion Awards, and *Time* magazine named him one of the "25 Most Influential Americans" in 1996.

Time magazine named him one of the "25 Most Influential Americans" in 1996.

On the down side, Calvin Klein, Inc., was forced to sell its successful underwear business because it needed the cash, and the company got caught up in another legal battle over the manufacture of its jeans. Calvin's personal life had also taken a downturn. In 1996, he and second wife Kelly separated, although they didn't divorce until 10 years later, and they remain good friends to this day.

In 1997, Calvin Klein, Inc., peaked at $5 billion in sales, half a billion of that in sales of Calvin Klein jeans—but two years later, the company found itself in trouble once again. This time, it couldn't recover. In 1999, Calvin Klein and Barry Schwartz put the company they'd created and nurtured up for sale.

In 2003, shirtmaker Phillips-Van Heusen purchased CKI.

A Focus on Fashion Photographers

There was a time when fashion photographers weren't considered "real" photographers. After all, didn't they just take pretty pictures of pretty models in pretty dresses? Wasn't it their job to snap shots to sell clothes in the Sears catalog?

Certainly, these types of photo shoots are still part of the job but, thanks to designers like Calvin Klein, fashion photography has become a well-respected art form, with thousands of up-and-coming photographers wanting to break into the biz.

This change in attitude toward photographers started in the late 1970s when fashion designers began taking risks in their advertising campaigns. Photographers and designers were suddenly partners in creating the images associated with fabulous fashion collections.

Richard Avedon was already a famous photographer when he teamed up with Calvin Klein and Brooke Shields to create the now-famous jeans ads. Steven Meisel, who worked with Calvin on one of his controversial ad campaigns, is credited with launching the careers of a number of supermodels, including Linda Evangelista, Naomi Campbell, and Christy Turlington. Bruce Weber, who has also worked with Ralph Lauren, helped define the Klein look to the public.

Other famous fashion photographers who have worked with Calvin include German-born Jurgen Teller, who has also worked with designers Vivienne Westwood and Marc Jacobs, Italian-born Mario Sorrenti, and American Irving Penn.

Chapter 6
Calvin Klein in the 21st Century— The Icon Steps Aside

W hen Calvin Klein and Barry Schwartz sold CKI on February 12, 2003, it marked the end of their 36-year partnership. Best friends since they'd met at age five, and best friends to the day the partnership ended, these boys from the Bronx have remained friends since then. But without the business to bind them, their lives have drifted in different directions.

Calvin designed his last collection, and took what would be his last bows on the runway, in September of 2003.

The Storm Before the Calm

For a few years, Calvin continued to be involved with the design side of the company that still bears his name, first as creative head, then as consulting creative director—a fancy name for an adviser. Barry retired from the fashion business the day the company was sold, redirecting his energies into his other passions in life—his family and horse racing.

Six weeks after Phillips-Van Heusen bought Calvin Klein's company, it was apparent that all was not well with the designer. During a basketball game at Madison Square Garden between the New York Knicks and the Toronto Raptors, Calvin wandered onto the court, mid-game. He approached a player who was about to throw the ball, grabbed his arm, and started chatting. A friend and a pair of security guards quickly escorted Calvin back to his courtside seat. He was clearly not himself.

It wasn't long before Calvin acknowledged he was, once again, struggling with drug and alcohol addiction, and he checked himself into a rehab clinic. "I crashed," he said a few years later. "I think I was overwhelmed with what was going to be next—the future."

He'd been planning for the sale of CKI for years, and he thought he was ready to let go of the business that had consumed his life for so long. "But when it actually happened, I just went completely crazy. Then, once again, I dealt with getting my life together. Since then, it's been the best time in my life."

Calvin designed his last collection, and took what would be his last bows on the runway, in September of 2003. He continued at his old

Designer Calvin Klein, President of Fashion Institute of Technology (FIT) Joyce Brown, and Vogue *magazine's editor in chief Anna Wintour pose before FIT's graduation ceremony at Radio City Music Hall on May 23, 2003, in New York City. Calvin was presented with an Honorary Doctor of Fine Arts degree at the FIT graduation ceremony.*

company, giving advice on collections and ad campaigns, until 2006.

Since then, he has kept himself out of the public eye, quietly spending time at, and renovating, his three homes—a mansion on Long Island, a penthouse in Manhattan, and a beach house in Miami, Florida. In fact, Calvin has become so publicity-shy, he didn't even attend the 2008 fashion show and party honoring the 40th anniversary of the company he founded.

The Legacy of Calvin Klein

Calvin Klein may now be living a quiet life out of the glare of the spotlight that shone on him for so long, but his name will remain in the limelight as long as his jeans, underwear, and fragrances are sold. To his everlasting credit is the fact that the fashion world has been forever changed because of his innovations to the industry.

cK one, a fragrance for males and females alike, ran an ad campaign featuring email addresses that customers could use to learn about the lives of the models shown in the ads. The idea, of course, was to stoke interest in the Calvin Klein brand, particularly among teenagers.

As America's first superstar designer, Calvin has also been one of its most enduring, sitting at the top of the fashion industry for almost 40 years. He was among the first to blaze his name on North American backsides with his designer jeans, the first to create women's underwear that looked like men's, and the first to make a unisex perfume, cK one. He was also the first to recognize the value of advertising that pushes the envelope.

Calvin changed the way fashion is marketed, beginning with the TV commercial that starred Brooke Shields and her body-hugging Calvin Klein jeans. His radical ads offended some people in the process—everyone from feminists to the mayor of New York City to the president of the United States. On the other hand, he has been hailed as a marketing genius who knew how to push the limits of social standards and, in doing so, kept his name in the news—and in front of the fashion-buying public.

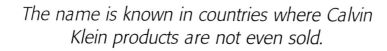

The name is known in countries where Calvin Klein products are not even sold.

CALVIN KLEIN, THE COMPANY, CONTINUES

After Calvin Klein took his final bows at the 2003 fashion show, he handed the creative reigns of the women's wear side of the company to Brazilian designer Francisco Costa. The menswear is now in the hands of Italo Zucchelli. Both men, now in their 40s, trained with Calvin, and both have earned CFDA Fashion Awards for their collections since taking over.

In 2004, the company bought the Internet domain name ck.com—one of the few two-letter domain names in existence. In 2006, it created a 600-seat permanent showroom—perfect for fashion shows—on the ground floor of the building that houses its headquarters. A year later, the company launched Calvin Klein Golf. Most major department stores now carry Calvin Klein lines, and boutiques have opened all over North America. In 2010, the company plans to open 60 new stores in China.

In a strange twist of business dealings, Phillips-Van Heusen, the company that owns the Calvin Klein name, purchased the Tommy Hilfiger label in March 2010. Hilfiger and Klein were great rivals in the past. Hilfiger even made a bid to buy Klein's company before Phillips-Van Heusen purchased it in 2003. Now, the two legacies live under one corporate roof.

Part of the Spring 2010 Calvin Klein collection. CKI partners Klein and Schwartz sold their company to Phillips-Van Heusen in 2003. Calvin stayed on with the company in a consulting capacity until 2006.

He created campaigns that thrilled young people and annoyed adults. He had a knack for knowing what would be the next big thing, and running with it.

Calvin was one of the first fashion designers to become a brand name, allowing other companies to use his identity to sell their products. His name is now on everything from shoes to hats, furniture to fabrics, and bath products to bed linens. The Calvin Klein name sells billions of dollars worth of clothing, accessories, and housewares every year. The name is known in countries where Calvin Klein products are not even sold.

Calvin has created clothing lines that appeal to hip teens and chic twenty-somethings—and their parents. Some of his creations are worthy of the red carpet; others are better suited to the boardroom or classroom. The Calvin Klein label might be on outerwear, or it might be on underwear. It is this wide appeal and broad range of products and styles that has made the man and his brand such a success.

Of course, Calvin is not without his critics. Some say he's more a copier than an innovator, a branding and marketing whiz rather than a designer. "Controversy has often surrounded Klein as much as celebrity," wrote Richard Martin, curator of the Costume Institute of the Metropolitan Museum of Art, in the *Modern Fashion Encyclopedia*. "But it is incontrovertible [undeniable] that Klein altered the landscape of modern American fashion and its perception as only a genius and a giant can."

In person, Calvin is a modest, even shy, individual who has remained true to the

The TV Reality of Fashion

In 2008, CKI signed on to sponsor *America's Next Top Male Model*, a so-called reality TV show inspired by the super-successful *America's Next Top Model*. The spin-off show didn't go anywhere, but the original series remains one of the biggest television hits ever.

Created and produced by supermodel—and super businesswoman—Tyra Banks, *America's Next Top Model* premiered in May 2003. While none of the winners have exactly become household names, the show certainly has. *ANTM* has been Number 1 in the U.S. ratings year after year, and it's shown in 170 countries around the world.

ANTM has also spawned 40 international versions of *Top Model* TV series, including those in Canada, Finland, and China, along with unexpected locales like Afghanistan, Israel, and West Africa. In spring 2010, when *ANTM* was in its 14th cycle of modelmaking, it was renewed for at least two more seasons.

The success of *Top Model* has likely been the inspiration for a number of related television reality shows: *Project Runway*, which has spun off into 13 different international versions; *Make Me a Supermodel*; *The Janice Dickinson Modeling Agency*, with former *ANTM* judge Dickinson; the short-lived *America's Most Smartest Model*; and *She's Got the Look: A Model Competition for Women Over 35*.

In March 2010, Calvin Klein creative director Francisco Costa had his moment in the reality TV spotlight as a guest judge on *Project Runway* alongside the show's regular judges, supermodel (and host) Heidi Klum, U.S. designer Michael Kors, and *Marie Claire* magazine's fashion director, Nina Garcia.

hardworking values his parents instilled in him 60-plus years ago. Calvin is a perfectionist whose discipline and drive have kept him focused on the task at hand. He has also had a knack for surrounding himself with talented people—beginning with Barry Schwartz, his financial whiz of a business partner—and giving them the freedom to do what they do best. Factor in Calvin's fearless pursuit of his fashion vision over the years, and it all adds up to a pretty potent recipe for success.

Said *New York Times* fashion critic Cathy Horyn in an article that ran just days before Calvin's final fashion show in 2003:

> *"He is the first American designer to become household-name famous.... Klein's genius was to shift the conversation from being one purely about fashion (what I wear) to attitude (how I look). And in doing that, he changed the whole game."*

Not bad for a boy from the Bronx who started designing clothes at age five.

THE ULTIMATE CLOSET

In the basement of Calvin Klein headquarters, in the Fashion District of New York City, is an archive of the designer's life work. Thousands of dresses, coats, and outfits from Calvin Klein collections from the 1960s to 2003 are stored here, simply hanging on racks in this giant underground closet.

Chronology

1942 Calvin Richard Klein is born in New York City, in the Bronx, on November 19.

1948 Calvin Klein meets Barry Schwartz, who would become his best friend and, later, his business partner.

1959–1962 Calvin attends the Fashion Institute of Technology, quitting after his first year, then returning to finish.

1962–1964 Calvin apprentices with coat-and-suit manufacturer Dan Millstein.

1964 Calvin marries Jayne Centre.

1964–1968 Calvin designs coats for Halldon, Inc., but creates his own line on the side.

1966 The Kleins' daughter Marci is born in October. He forms Calvin Klein Ltd. with partner Barry Schwartz.

1968 Calvin sets up a showroom in the York Hotel, where he is discovered by Don O'Brien who introduces him to Mildred Custin, president of the Bonwit Teller department store chain.

1969 Calvin is featured on the cover of *Vogue* magazine for the first time.

1973 Calvin designs his first line of women's sportswear, creating what would become known as the "Calvin Klein Look." He wins the first of three-in-a-row Coty Awards.

1974 Calvin and Jayne Centre divorce in August.

1976 Calvin launches a line of designer jeans. They flop.

1978 He launches a better-quality, better-fitting, this time successful line of designer jeans. In March, 11-year-old Marci Klein is kidnapped, held for nine hours, and released unharmed. Calvin launches his first menswear collection.

1980 The Brooke Shields TV commercial debuts.

1982 Calvin launches his line of underwear.

1981 He hires Kelly Rector as design assistant.

1982 He wins the first of six Council of Fashion Designers of America (CFDA) Fashion Awards.

1985 Calvin launches Obsession perfume. In the 1990s, the ad campaign will feature British model Kate Moss.

1986 He marries Kelly Rector in Italy.

1988 Calvin enters a rehab clinic for drug and alcohol abuse.

1992 Calvin's company is on the verge of bankruptcy. His friend and record producer David Geffen saves the company with a $62 million loan. Underwear ads showing rapper Marky Mark (Mark Wahlberg) in nothing but his Calvins debut.

1993 Calvin launches cK, a clothing line aimed at younger, hipper shoppers. That same year, he is named America's Best Designer.

1994 The unauthorized biography *Obsession: The Lives and Times of Calvin Klein* is published.

1995 A controversial cK ad campaign featuring young-looking models is pulled after a public outcry.

1996 *Time* magazine names Calvin Klein to its list of 25 Most Influential Americans. Calvin and his second wife separate. They don't divorce until 2006.

1999 Another controversial ad campaign is pulled after public outcry. Calvin and Barry Schwartz put Calvin Klein, Inc., up for sale.

2001 Calvin earns a Lifetime Achievement Award from the Council of Fashion Designers of America (CFDA).

2003 Shirtmaker Phillips-Van Heusen buys CKI on February 12 for a total of $435 million. Six weeks later, Calvin approaches a basketball player, mid-game, at an NBA game at Madison Square Garden and is escorted back to his seat. In April, he enters a rehab clinic for drug and alcohol abuse. In September, he attends his final runway show featuring his final collection.

2008 CKI stages a fashion show and party honoring the 40th anniversary of the company. Calvin Klein does not attend.

Glossary

airbrushed In advertising and magazine photos, having blemishes removed and other features softened or changed to enhance one's appearance

avant-garde Artistically innovative or experimental

brand name A product made and named by a particular company. Kleenex, for example, is the brand name of a particular facial tissue. Coke and Pepsi are the brand names of cola drinks.

charmeuse A lightweight fabric with a satin finish on one side and a dull finish on the other

double-knit A firm, heavyweight, slightly stretchy fabric that looks the same on both sides

faux fur Fake fur made to look like real fur

flagship store The main, often biggest, most important store in a chain

gabardine A tough fabric, smooth on one side, with narrow, diagonal ribs on the other, usually wool or cotton, used to make suits, coats, and pants

gamine A girl or young woman who looks boyish

grande dame An important, usually older woman, well respected in her field

Harlem A largely African-American neighborhood in Manhattan

haute couture A French term that literally means "high sewing"; expensive, fancy clothing designed and custom-fit for a specific person

innovation A new method, idea, or product

made-to-order Clothing custom-made for a specific person

mannequin A life-sized model of a human figure used to display clothing in stores

mix-and-match separates A collection of clothing pieces that can be worn together in various combinations—for example, a set that includes pants, a skirt, a T-shirt, and a blouse

muse A person who inspires another person's creativity

notions Small items used in sewing, such as needles, thread, pins, and buttons

paparazzi Photographers who follow famous people to get

newsworthy and especially, shocking or embarrassing photos

polyester A strong, synthetic fabric that is easy to care for and doesn't wear out easily

posh Elegant, stylish, or high-class

power suit A woman's suit with wide shoulders and sharp lines, made of rigid fabric; popular in the 1980s to make businesswomen fit in better with businessmen

protégé A young person who is being trained by someone older, experienced, and influential in a particular field

publicist A person responsible for publicizing or promoting something or someone

quintessence The best example of something

radical Extreme or revolutionary

rayon A soft, flowing, lightweight fabric used mostly for blouses, skirts, and dresses

ready-to-wear Also called off-the-rack; mass-produced clothing made in standard sizes to fit most people without much alteration

royalty, royalties Money paid on every sale of a product to the person or company who created it; money paid on every sale for the right to use a famous name, like Calvin Klein, on the product

shoulder pads Pads sewn into suits and dresses to give the garment a more square shape

signature (as in signature fragrance or signature style) A distinctive characteristic that identifies the fragrance or style with a particular individual

society columnist A newspaper writer who writes about who is doing what in the community; sometimes called a gossip columnist

sportswear Casual clothing

trade magazine A publication dedicated to a particular type of business or industry

trendsetter One who leads or sets the pace for fashion

tweed A rough, itchy, heavy woven wool fabric usually used for overcoats and suits

twill A strong woven fabric with diagonal ridges or ribs on its surface. Denim is an example of a twill fabric.

unauthorized biography The life story of a celebrity who has not given permission for the story to be written. It often contains questionable information.

unisex Suitable for either gender

waif A person who looks thin, young, and unhealthy

Further Information

Books

Beker, Jeanne. *Passion for Fashion: Careers in Style*.
Toronto: Tundra Books, 2008.

Marsh, Lisa. *The House of Klein: Fashion, Controversy, and a Business Obsession*. Hoboken, NJ: John Wiley & Sons, Inc., 2003.

Montero, Gabriel. *A Stitch in Time: A History of New York's Fashion District*. Fashion Center Business Improvement District, 2008.

Tucker, Andrew, and Tamsin Kingswell. *Fashion: A Crash Course*. Vancouver: Raincoast Books, 2000.

Online

WEB SITES:
http://www.fashionencyclopedia.com
This site provides profiles of dozens of fashion designers, including Calvin Klein, Claire McCardell, and Jacques Tiffeau. It also features information on fashion through the ages, from around the world. The Modern World section looks at specific elements of 20th century fashion, decade by decade.

http://www.fashionincubator.com/resources/becoming_a_designer/fashion_schools_canada.shtml
This site, compiled by Toronto Fashion Incubator, gives a list of fashion schools in Canada, along with contact information.

http://fuzzylizzie.com/fashionsfinest.html
Created by Lizzie Bramlett, this site profiles fashion designers of days gone by, including Claire McCardell. Also on the Fuzzylizzie Vintage Clothing site are great vintage fashion photos, articles about trends, and specific fashion pieces through the ages.

**www.fashionwindows.com/fashion_designers/
showall_fashion_designers.asp**
This site, called Fashion Windows, lists hundreds of fashion designers, with articles and bios about them. The list includes companies, not just individual designers.

**http://www.fashionwindows.com/fashion_designers/
calvin_klein/default.asp**
This is the Fashion Windows page about Calvin Klein.

**http://www.evancarmichael.com/Famous-Entrepreneurs/
557/summary.php**
Titled Famous Entrepreneur Advice, this site provides insights from dozens of successful business people in all different professions and industries. In the Fashion & Cosmetics category, for example, 15 entrepreneurs are represented, including Calvin Klein. The Calvin Klein page then leads to quotes and motivational advice from the designer about specific topics, and biographical information.

**http://watch.fashiontelevision.com/
fashion-icons/designers/calvin-klein/#clip105965**
Fashion Television is a great resource for anyone interested in the world of fashion. With links to videos about designers, runway shows, and other fashion events, there's a lot to look at. This particular link will take you to a short video about the Calvin Klein 40th anniversary party in September 2008.

http://cityfile.com/profiles/calvin-klein
This site is full of profiles of famous people who live in New York. It has facts and figures, along with some trivia and gossip.

ONLINE ARTICLE:
Horyn, Cathy. "Style; The Calvinistic Ethic," *The New York Times*, September 14, 2003. **www.nytimes.com/2003/09/14/
magazine/style-the-calvinist-ethic.html?pagewanted=all**

Index

1980s, the 75-76, 77, 78

advertising controversies 65-66, 70, 84, 86, 88-89, 97
America's Next Top Model 101
awards 9, 57, 61, 76, 89

Back to the Future 71
Banks, Jeffrey 57, 60-61
Bonwit Teller 6, 46, 47, 48, 51-52, 54-56
boutiques 80, 98
branding 10, 61-62, 63, 89, 100
Brown, Joyce 95

Calvin Klein Golf 98
Calvin Klein Home 89
Calvin Klein, Inc. (CKI) 49, 64, 78-79, 90, 93, 96
    continued involvement with 94, 96
    financial difficulties 79, 80, 90
    new creative control 98
    selling the business 90, 93, 94
Calvin Klein Look, The 8, 56
Calvin Klein Ltd. 48, 51-52
Cardin, Pierre 32, 47
celebrities 59

Brooke Shields 65, 66, 67, 91, 97
Centre, Jayne 24, 38, 39, 40, 62
charity fashion shows 55
childhood 13-14, 16-18, 19, 20, 22
cK fashion line 80, 82, 86, 88
CKI *see* Calvin Klein, Inc. (CKI)
Clinton, President Bill 88
Clueless 81
coats 30, 40-42, 46, 48, 51, 61
collections 5, 7, 46, 56, 78, 80, 94, 98, 99
    in Bonwit Teller 52, 54
copper rivets 10
Council of Fashion Designers of America (CFDA)
    Fashion Awards 61, 76, 89, 98
    Lifetime Achievement Award 9
Courrèges, André 47
Custin, Mildred 6, 47, 48, 52, 54
cutting patterns and fabric 29-30

Dan Millstein, Inc. 30, 32, 34-36
darker side of business 35
Dean, James 10, 11
designer labels 32, 58

designing clothing 40-42, 44
    in childhood 16-17
Dinah's Place 55
Dior, Christian 23, 25, 32
dresses 42, 46
drug and alcohol abuse 73, 78, 94

early jobs 18, 22, 29-30, 32, 34-36
education 18
    fashion schools 27
    high school 20, 21, 22
    public school 18, 19, 20
eveningwear 9

fabrics used 8, 23, 25, 40, 41
family
    daughter Marci 39, 40, 62, 68, 69, 80, 82
    father Leo 13, 14, 17, 18, 45
    grandmother Molly Stern 14, 15, 16
    helping out 51
    mother Flore (Flo) 13-14, 16, 17, 38
    wife Jayne Centre 24, 38, 39, 40, 62
    wife Kelly Rector 72-73, 90
Fashion District 27, 33, 49, 55, 103
    see also Garment District

Fashion Institute of Technology (FIT) 21, 22, 95
fashion photographers 91
fashion shows 6, 60-61, 82, 96
Fashion Week 7, 83
financial difficulties 45, 79, 80, 90
first big order 48, 51-52
fitness 75-76, 77
fragrances 70, 77-78, 84, 96, 97

Garment District 21, 31, 33, 41, 49
see also Fashion District
Geffen, David 79, 80
grocery business
    Leo Klein's 14, 45
    Schwartz family's 18, 43, 44
Gunn, Tim, 27

Halldon Ltd. 40-41, 42
Harper's Bazaar 55
High School of Industrial Art 20, 22, 24
Hilfiger, Tommy 83, 98
home décor collection 89
honorary degree 95

importing clothing 32
income 54, 64, 65, 90
influences 15, 16, 22, 100, 102
Internet domain 98

jeans 8, 62, 64-65, 66, 78, 90, 97
    copper rivets on 10

Gloria Vanderbilt 64, 65
Levi Strauss 10

Karan, Donna 83
Klein, Marci 39, 40, 62, 80, 82
    kidnapping 68, 69

labels 5, 10, 64
Lauren, Ralph 19, 72, 83, 91
legacy 96-97, 100, 102
legal battles 78, 90
licensing 61-62, 63, 89, 100
logo-wear 60, 97

made-to-order clothing 30
magazines 55
Mark, Marky 84, 86
McCardell, Claire 22, 23, 27
media attention 56, 76, 78
menswear 66, 70, 78, 80, 98
Missy clothing 34
mix-and-match separates, 23, 106
models
    supermodels 76, 77, 91
    too-skinny 84, 85, 87, 88
Moss, Kate 84, 85
movies brand appeared in 71, 81

"**N**eedle Threading a Button" sculpture 32, 33
New York City 49

O'Brien, Don 48

Paltrow, Gwyneth 59
Paris 32, 35-36
personal style 20
Phillips-Van Heusen 90, 94, 98
production 51-52
Project Runway 27, 101
publicity 55-56, 86, 96, 97
Puritan Fashions 64

ready-to-wear clothing 25
Rebel Without a Cause 10, 11
Rector, Kelly 72-73, 90
rivals 83, 98
runway shows 35-36, 94

Schwartz, Barry
    business partner 44, 45-46, 51-52, 53, 60, 64, 78, 90, 93, 94
    friendship with 18, 20, 44, 93
    grocery business 43, 44
Shields, Brooke 65, 66, 67, 91, 97
Shlansky, Louis 40, 41, 46
simplicity 48, 59
sketching 20, 34, 36, 37
sportswear 9, 56, 57
stores 80, 89, 98
    Bonwit Teller 6, 46, 47, 48, 51-52, 54-56
    department stores 83, 98
Strauss, Levi 10
Studio 54 62, 64, 67, 72

Index

T-shirts 8, 60-61, 66
teenager market 10, 86,
   96, 100
television reality shows
   101
The New York Times 54
Tiffeau, Jacques 22, 25
Tobe Report 41-42
TV shows 55

underground closet 103
underwear 8, 66, 70, 84,
   86, 88-89, 90
Ungaro, Emanuel 47

Vanderbilt, Gloria 64, 65
Vogue 55, 62, 95

wages 29, 34, 40
Wagner, Faye 32, 34
Wahlberg, Mark (aka
   Marky Mark) 84, 86
window displays 54
Wintour, Anna 95
Women's Wear Daily 22,
   58

York Hotel showrooms
   5-6, 9, 33, 43, 46
young adult clothing 80,
   82, 100

About the Author

Diane Dakers was born and raised in Toronto and now makes her home in Victoria, British Columbia, Canada. A specialist in Canadian arts and cultural issues, Diane has been a newspaper, magazine, television, and radio journalist since 1991. She loves finding and telling stories about what makes people tick—be they celebrities like Calvin Klein, or not-so-famous folks like you and me. This is Diane's first book, and Calvin Klein is one of her favorite designers. She has been known to wear CK socks, underwear, and perfume.